TABLE OF CONTENTS

WINNING HIS FIRST TITLE

John Cena was confident as he walked into the ring at *WrestleMania* in 2004. He was going against wrestler Big Show for his first World Wrestling Entertainment (WWE) championship. John's confidence faded when Big Show began tossing him around. After a few minutes, John was lying stunned on the floor.

FACT

Big Show weighs nearly 500 pounds (227 kilograms).
That's about twice as much as John.

Big Show pushed, pounded, and kicked John. But John wouldn't give up. At last he got a solid punch in. Then John picked up Big Show and slammed him to the floor for the **pin**. John Cena was the new United States Champion!

pin—when a wrestler is held firmly on his back for a certain length of time

WRESTLING DREAMS

John Felix Anthony Cena was born on April 23, 1977, in West Newbury, Massachusetts. As a boy he watched pro wrestling with his father, John Cena Sr. John and his four brothers enjoyed wrestling each other. John pretended to be pro wrestling star Hulk Hogan.

FACT

As a kid John made a wrestling championship belt out of paper. He still has it!

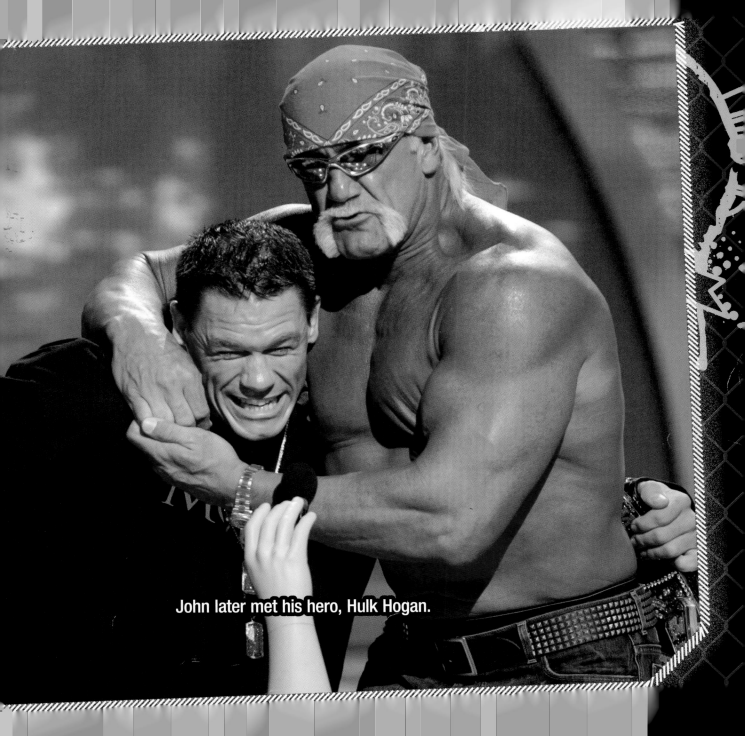

John later met his hero, Hulk Hogan.

John and Randy Orton face off in a 2008 match.

Orton's Time Is up!

FACT

While training to be a pro wrestler John became friends with Randy Orton. Both men went on to become WWE stars.

When John was young, he was skinny. At age 13 John began lifting weights. He grew larger and stronger. John was a good athlete in high school and college. After college he worked in a gym. He also began training to be a pro wrestler. In 2001 John signed a **development contract** with WWE.

development contract—a deal in which a wrestler is paid to compete in a smaller league as a way to train for a bigger league like WWE

BECOMING A STAR

When John started wrestling for WWE, he went by his real name. His **gimmick** was acting like a loud-mouthed hip-hop rapper. Fans loved it! John soon became WWE's most popular **babyface**.

TRIBUTE TO THE TROOPS

WWE has been holding *Tribute to the Troops* since 2003. WWE wrestlers have visited U.S. military troops in Iraq and Afghanistan. John has taken part in nine of the 10 shows.

gimmick—a clever trick or idea used to get people's attention

babyface—a wrestler who acts as a hero in the ring

After John earned his first championship in 2004, he had a **custom** belt made. His design had a spinning center plate with an American flag background. John lost his belt in a match against Orlando Jordan on March 3, 2005. Jordan destroyed the belt. He replaced it with the original WWE U.S. Championship belt.

custom—specially done or made

John's first championship wasn't his last. He has also won the WWE championship and the World Heavyweight championship. John wrestled in **tag teams** too. He has won the WWE Tag Team championship and the World Tag Team championship.

tag team—when two wrestlers partner together against other teams

FACT

The only big title John hasn't won is the Intercontinental Championship.

John in the 2006 movie *The Marine*

John found fame in pro wrestling, but that's not his only talent. John has written and performed music. He has starred in movies. He also enjoys working on cars. John owns a large collection of cars.

MAKING WISHES COME TRUE

John is proud to be a part of the Make-A-Wish Foundation. This organization grants wishes to kids with life-threatening illnesses. Many kids wish to meet celebrities. In 2013 John granted his 300th wish!

FUTURE PLANS

What does the future hold for John Cena? More movies? Music? Or perhaps he'll finally chase down the Intercontinental Championship. With any luck, John will be a WWE fan favorite for years to come.

TIMELINE

1977 – John Felix Anthony Cena is born on April 23.

1990 – John starts lifting weights.

2001 – John signs on with WWE.

2004 – John defeats Big Show to win the United States Championship.

2005 – John releases his first musical album, *You Can't See Me.*

2006 – John stars in his first feature film, *The Marine.*

2008 – John defeats Chris Jericho to become the World Heavyweight Champion.

2010 – John wins his first WWE Tag Team Championship with David Otunga.

2013 – John wins the WWE Championship for the 11th time. It's the most times the title has ever been held by a wrestler.

GLOSSARY

babyface (BAY-bee-fayss)—a wrestler who acts as a hero in the ring

championship (CHAM-pee-uhn-ship)—a contest or final game of a series that determines which team or player will be the overall winner

custom (KUHS-tuhm)—specially done or made

development contract (duh-VEHL-up-ment KAHN-tract)—a deal in which a wrestler is paid to compete in a smaller league as a way to train for a bigger league like WWE

gimmick (GIM-ik)—a clever trick or idea used to get people's attention

pin (PIN)—when a wrestler is held firmly on his back for a certain length of time

tag team (TAG TEEM)—when two wrestlers partner together against other teams

READ MORE

Nagelhout, Ryan. *John Cena.* Superstars of Wrestling. New York: Gareth Stevens, 2013.

Shields, Brian. *John Cena.* DK Readers. New York: DK, 2009.

Weil, Ann. *Pro Wrestling Greats.* The Best of the Best. Mankato, Minn.: Capstone Press, 2012.

INTERNET SITES

FactHound offers a safe, fun way to find Internet sites related to this book. All of the sites on FactHound have been researched by our staff.

Here's all you do:

Visit *www.facthound.com*

Type in this code: 9781476542072

Super-cool stuff! Check out projects, games and lots more at **www.capstonekids.com**

INDEX